INCOMPLETE RECORDS

Revision Workbook

Teresa Clarke FMAAT

INCOMPLETE RECORDS

BY TERESA CLARKE FMAAT

Chapter 1 - Introduction

I have written this workbook to assist students who are studying bookkeeping or accountancy. It is designed as a revision workbook to complement your studies and help you master some tricky topics. I hope it will help you to consolidate your studies so that you can become more confident with this subject and enable you to feel more comfortable with the exam questions.

The construction of financial statements from incomplete records is occasionally applied in real life situations.

A variety of techniques can be used to reconstruct the financial records and we will be looking at some of these in this workbook, including mark-up and margin, bank account reconstruction, net assets approach, SLCA and PLCA ledgers and the VAT control account. Each of these will be covered in this workbook.

The reconstruction of financial information from incomplete records is an essential element of the AAT Level 3 qualification unit of Final Accounts for Sole Traders and Partnerships and Level 3 synoptic (AQ2016), Final Accounting: Preparing Financial Statements (Q2022), as well as other bookkeeping and accounting qualifications.

This workbook will take you through examples with worked answers and then give you some tasks to work through on your own, with answers given at the end of the book.

The DEAD CLIC rules can be applied to incomplete records, and I will be referring to these throughout the workbook. Here is a reminder of the rule.

Debits increase

Expenses

Assets

Drawings

Credits increase

Liabilities

Income

Capital

Make a note of this or perhaps make a flashcard, as you will be using this quite a bit through your studies.

Businesses generally keep good accounting records including bank statements, copy invoices, receipts, till rolls, journals, records of invoices sent, etc. and these are recorded in either a manual accounting system, on spreadsheets or using accounting software such as Sage, Xero or QuickBooks.

Occasionally records may not be available for several reasons, including fire, theft, or computer problems.

Sometimes information is missing because a business has failed to keep details, such as drawings or inventory.

Exam style questions will ask you to find missing figures from the information provided using a variety of techniques.

The techniques that are used include those which we will look at in this workbook:
- The net assets approach
- Control account reconstruction
- Mark-up and margin
- Cash and bank accounts

The net assets approach

When using the net assets approach, we use the accounting equation:

Net assets = capital (in its simplest form)

Assets – liabilities = net assets

Assets – liabilities = capital plus profit less drawings

Note: You need to remember this equation for your studies.

We can use this to find the amount of capital that has been introduced:

An increase in net assets = capital introduced plus profit less drawings

We can also use it to find a missing drawings figure:

Net assets = capital plus profit less drawings

In an example this could be written like this:

Net assets £50,000 = Capital £40,000 + Profit £30,000 - Drawings £?

£50,000 = £40,000 + £30,000 - ?

£50,000 = £40,000 + £30,000 - £20,000

Don't worry if this sounds a little confusing, we will look at some example tasks.

INCOMPLETE RECORDS

Example 1

Vinegar Supplies has provided you with their accounting records and this includes a list of assets and liabilities, but they have given you no details of the drawings taken out of the business during the year.

Assets total	£93,000
Liabilities total	£41,000
Capital	£50,000 (no changes during the year)
Profit for the year	£34,000

Now we can construct the accounting equation from this information:

93 − 41 = 52

Assets − liabilities = net assets

£93,000 − £41,000 = £52,000

52   50 + 34 − 32

Net assets = capital plus profit less drawings

£52,000 = capital + profit − drawings

£52,000 = £50,000 + £34,000 − ?

£52,000 = £50,000 + £34,000 − £32,000

Workings: If you are unsure of how to calculate that final step try this on your calculator.

Take the answer of £52,000, then reverse the positive and negative numbers.

£52,000 - £50,000 - £34,000 = -£32,000

By taking the positive numbers and turning them into negatives, the answer here gives a negative which is what we add to the end of the equation as a "*minus drawings*".

£52,000 = £50,000 + £34,000 - £32,000

INCOMPLETE RECORDS

An exam question will not always total the assets and liabilities for you, so you need to be confident that you can work through a list to identify these. Let's look at another example:

Example 2

Barry Battery has provided us with a list of assets and liabilities at the start of the year and a list of assets and liabilities at the end of the year. Barry Battery does not have a record of his drawings for the year, so we need to use the net assets approach to find this.

Ledger account	Balance at 1 Jan 2020 £	Balance at 31 Dec 2020 £
Delivery vans	A 10,000	20,000
Sales ledger control account	A 14,000	22,000
Bank balance (money in bank)	A 1,000	6,000
Purchase ledger control account	L 4,000	5,000
Bank loan outstanding	L 4,000	2,000

We are told that the profit for the year ended 31 December 2020 is £36,000.

[handwritten: 10 + 14 + 1 = 25 − 8 = 17 net asset]

We need to find the missing drawing figure from this information, so we use the accounting equation again.

INCOMPLETE RECORDS

Assets – liabilities = capital + profit – drawings

We need to identify which of the list are assets and which are liabilities. I have marked each with an A for asset and an L for liability in the table below. Make sure that you are confident in identifying these before moving on.

Remember that assets are things that the business owns or are owed to it, and liabilities are things that the business owes to others.

	Ledger account	Balance at 1 Jan 2020 £	Balance at 1 Jan 2020 £
A	Delivery vans	10,000	20,000
A	Sales ledger control account	14,000	22,000
A	Bank balance (money in bank)	1,000	6,000
L	Purchase ledger control account	4,000	5,000
L	Bank loan outstanding	4,000	2,000

Assets – liabilities = capital + profit – drawings

We can calculation the net assets at the start of the year and at the end of the year.

INCOMPLETE RECORDS

At the start of the year, we had the following figures (taken from the table above).

£25,000 (assets) - £8,000 (liabilities) = £17,000 (net assets)

At the end of the year, we had the following figures.

£48,000 (assets) - £7,000 (liabilities) = £41,000 (net assets)

To find the increase in net assets, we take the closing net assets figure and take this away from the opening net assets figure (both calculated above). £17,000 to £41,000 = £24,000 increase.

There is an increase in the net assets from £17,000 to £41,000, an increase of £24,000.

Increase in net assets = capital at the start of the year + profit for the year – drawings

£24,000 = £17,000 + £36,000 - ?

£24,000 = £17,000 + £36,000 - £29,000

To find that missing figure remember to put in the answer first, £24,000, then reverse the positive and negative numbers.

Workings: £24,000 – 17,000 – 36,000 = -£29,000

The missing figure of £29,000 is the drawings for the year.

INCOMPLETE RECORDS

Example 3

We could use a similar method if the profit figure was missing, or indeed the net assets figure. We can look at these in a table.

Net assets £	Capital £	Profit £	Drawings £
60,000	50,000	40,000	30,000
44,000	30,000	20,000	6000
25,000	5000	32,000	12,000
47,000	40,000	15,000	8,000

We can use maths to work out the missing numbers. I will show you my method, but if you have a different way and get to the correct answer, stick to your own method. There is no correct way, just the way that works for you.

Net assets £	Capital £	Profit £	Drawings £
60,000	50,000	**40,000**	30,000
44,000	30,000	20,000	**6,000**
25,000	**5,000**	32,000	12,000
47,000	40,000	15,000	8,000

INCOMPLETE RECORDS

Workings:

60,000 – 50,000 - ? + 30,000 (Remember to reverse the positive or negative numbers in the equation)

Net assets of 60,000 – 50,000 + 30,000 - ?
60,000 – 50,000 + 30,000 = 40,000

Net assets of 44,000 – 30,000 – 20,000 = -6000 (This is a minus number because the equation says 'less drawings').

Net assets of 25,000 – 32,000 + 12,000 = 5,000

Capital of 40,000 + 15,000 – 8,000 = 47,000

Cash and bank ledgers

We can find missing figures using the bank or cash ledgers, such as the sales for the period, by reconstructing the ledgers. We can look at this in an example.

Example 4

Mavis Black runs a market stall but has not kept a record of her sales. All her sales are cash sales. She has provided us with the following information about her business.

Cash at the start of the year	£250
Cash at the end of the year	£380
Cash banked during the year	£14,200
Expenses paid by cash	£4,300

We can reconstruct the cash account with the above figures to calculate the missing sales figure:

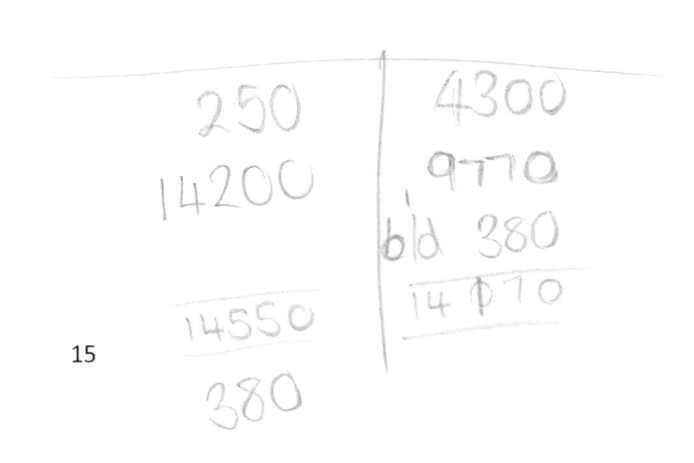

Cash account

Debit	£	Credit	£
Balance b/d	250	Bank	14,200
	18630	Expenses	4,300
		Balance c/d	380

DEAD CLIC is applied here to ensure that entries are made on the correct sides.

The balance b/d is a debit because this is an asset. Cash is something that is owned by the business.

The bank entry is a credit because this is money that came out of this cash account and into the bank as a debit.

The expenses are a credit because they were paid out of the cash account and are a debit in the expenses account, because expenses are a debit according to DEAD CLIC..

The balance c/d is a credit because this will be brought down as a debit in the next period as an asset.

Now we can find the missing figure, the sales figure.

Sales will be a debit in the cash account and a credit in the sales account.

This is because the cash account is an asset, and this is increasing with the cash sales. More money is going into the 'cash pot', so increasing the asset.

The sales account will be a credit as this is a form of income according to DEAD CLIC.

It is useful to draw up the opposite accounts to avoid errors, even if they are not needed as part of the task. I have shown these below the answer.

Cash account

Debit	£	Credit	£
Balance b/d	250	Bank	14,200
Sales	*18,630*	Expenses	4,300
		Balance c/d	380
	18,880		18,880
Balance b/d	380		

Sales

Debit	£	Credit	£
		Cash	18,630

Bank

Debit	£	Credit	£
Cash	14,200		

Expenses

Debit	£	Credit	£
Cash	4,300		

SLCA and PLCA reconstruction

If the sales or purchases figures are missing, then you can use this approach. It can also be used to find other items, such as discounts received or allowed, that appear in the sales ledger control account or purchase ledger control account.

Before looking at this example, it is a good time to remind ourselves about the typical contents of the sales ledger control account or receivables.

The balance b/d in the sales ledger control account will be on the debit side as this is the amount owed to the business. This account is also known as the trade receivables account. It may also be abbreviated to SLCA.

The only other entry on the debit side is the new credit sales which increase what is owed to the business.

On the credit side of the SLCA we have items which reduce what is owed to the business, such as sales returns, money received from customers, discounts allowed, irrecoverable debts and contra entries. If you remember that the only two debit entries are the balance b/d and new credit sales, it will be much easier to reconstruct.

INCOMPLETE RECORDS

Sales ledger control account / Trade receivables

Debit	£	Credit	£
Balance b/d		Sales returns	
Sales		Bank (from customers)	
		Discounts allowed	
		Irrecoverable debts	
		Contra entries with PLCA	

A similar set of contents will exist for the purchase ledger control account or payables.

The balance b/d in the purchase ledger control account will be on the credit side as this is the amount owed by the business to its suppliers. This account is also known as the trade payables account. It may also be abbreviated to PLCA.

The only other entry on the credit side will be new credit purchases which increase the amount that the business owes to its suppliers.

On the debit side we have items which reduce the amount owed to suppliers, such as purchase returns, discounts received, bank payments made and contra entries.

If you remember that the only two credit entries are the balance b/d and new credit purchases, it will be much easier to reconstruct.

Purchase ledger control account / Trade payables

Debit	£	Credit	£
Purchase returns		Balance b/d	
Discounts received		Purchases	
Bank (payments made)			
Contra entry to SLCA			

Example 5

Ollie Ginger has provided you with the following information about his sales but has not kept a record of the discounts allowed to his customers. We can use the information below to reconstruct the SLCA to find the missing figure.

Sales	£46,500
Payments received from customers	£38,000
Balance b/d (at start of period)	£4,800
Sales returns	£1,800
Balance c/d (at end of period)	£5,600

We can reconstruct the SLCA to find the missing discounts allowed figure.

The balance b/d is a debit because the SLCA account is an asset. Remember that the only other debit will be more sales. Everything else is a credit entry.

We enter the balance b/d on the debit side as a credit, along with new credit sales that increase the amount of money that customers owe the business.

We enter the sales returns as a credit because they reduce the amount of money that customers owe us.

We enter the bank payments received from customers as a credit because this reduces the amount that the customers owe us.

We enter the discounts allowed in, without a figure as this is missing, but we know that this will reduce what the customers owe the business.

We enter the balance c/d on the credit side, because this will be brought down in the next period on the debit side as an asset, money owed to the business.

SLCA

Debit	£	Credit	£
Balance b/d	4,800	Sales returns	1,800
Sales	46,500	Bank (from customers)	38,000
		Discounts allowed	?
		Balance c/d	5,600

INCOMPLETE RECORDS

We balance the account to find the missing number by totalling the highest side, the debit side in this case, putting the total at the bottom. Enter the same number on the bottom of the credit side, take away all the other numbers and the number you are left with is the missing discounts allowed figure.

Sales Ledger Control Account / Receivables

Debit	£	Credit	£
Balance b/d	4,800	Sales returns	1,800
Sales	46,500	Bank (from customers)	38,000
		Discounts allowed	**5,900**
		Balance c/d	5,600
	51,300		51,300

Remember:

SLCA

The only debit entries are the balance b/d and new credit sales; all the rest are credits.

PLCA

The only credit entries are the balance b/d and new credit purchases; all the rest are debits.

Now you can reconstruct a SLCA or PLCA and find any missing figure. You will be able to try this in the tasks that lay ahead in the next chapter.

Mark-up and margin

Mark-up is on cost and takes the cost figure of 100% and marks <u>UP</u>.

Margin is within sales and take the sales figure of 100% and the margin is with<u>IN</u> this.

So, mark-up goes up from 100% and margin is within 100%.

The best way to approach this type of question is with a table and I would always recommend that you draw this for mark-up and margin questions.

Example 6

Jas buys units for £250 each and uses mark-up at 25% to set his sale price. Calculate the sales price for Jas.

First fill in what you know.

Mark-up table

Cost	100%	£250
Mark-up	25%	62 50
Sales price	125%	312 50

When using mark-up, we start with the cost price and go up from, so cost is 100%.

Mark-up table

Cost	100%	£250
Mark-up	25%	62 50
Sales price	125%	312 50

Now we can fill in the rest of the table with some maths.

If the cost is £250 and this represents 100%, we can work out 1% by dividing the cost by the total percentage.

£250 / 100 = £2.50

1% = £2.50

Now we know that 1% is £2.50, we can find the mark-up of 25%, but multiplying £2.50 by 25.

£2.50 x 25 = £62.50

The sales price is the cost of the item plus the mark-up.

100% + 25% = 125%

£250 + £62.50 = £312.50

To check this, we can multiply £2.50 x 125 for the sales price.

£2.50 x 125 = £312.50

Mark-up table

Cost	100%	£250
Mark-up	25%	£62.50
Sales price	125%	£312.50

Example 7

Janis buys units for £140 each and uses margin at 30% to work out her sales price. Calculate the sales price for Janis.

First fill in what you know.

Margin table

Cost	100 70	£140
Margin	30%	
Sales price	100	

When using margin this is within the sales price, so the sales price is 100%.

140/70%

Margin table

Cost	70	£140
Margin	30%	42 60
Sales price	100%	182 200

INCOMPLETE RECORDS

We know the sales price is 100% and the margin is 30%, so remembering that this is all withIN 100%, the cost must be 70%.

100 − 30 = 70.

We know the cost is £140 and this represents 70%, so we can find the value of 1% by dividing the cost by the percentage.

£140 / 70 = £2

1% = £2

Now we know the value of 1%, we can multiply this by 30 to find the margin.

£2 x 30 = £60

And by 100 to find the sale price

£2 x 100 = £200

To check this, we can add the cost to the margin to find the sales price.

£140 + £60 = £200

Margin table

Cost	70%	£140
Margin	30%	£60
Sales price	100%	£200

Example 8

Ingrida has told us that she uses a mark-up percentage of 40% on her sales. She has also told us that the sales price is £700. Calculate the cost of goods sales figure from this information.

We always start by drawing up the table with the information we know.

Mark-up table

Cost	100%	~~700~~ 500
Mark-up	40%	~~280~~ 200
Sales price	140%	£700 / 140%

We know that mark-up is on cost as cost is the 100% and we go up from that. We can enter in the percentages.

Mark-up table

Cost	100%	
Mark-up	40%	
Sales price	140%	£700

To find the missing numbers now we take the £700 and divide it by its associated percentage of 140 to find 1%.

£700 / 140 = £5

£5 = 1%

Mark-up is 40% so we multiply £5 by 40 to find this figure.

£5 x 40 = £200

The cost is 100% so we multiply £5 by 100 to find this figure.

£5 x 100 = £500

When we put these in the table, we can check the figures:

Mark-up table

Cost	100%	**£500**
Mark-up	40%	**£200**
Sales price	140%	£700

To check this we take the cost and add the mark-up to find the sales price

£500 + £200 = £700

Example 9

Temitope has told us that the sales price for her product is £90, and she has told us that the margin used to calculate this was 18%. Calculate the cost of sales figure from this information.

We draw the margin table first and put in the information we know.

Margin table

Cost	100	~~100~~ ~~72~~ 73 80
Margin	18%	16 20
Sales price	82	£90

Margin means within 100%, so we know that the sale figure is 100% and the other figures are both within 100%.

Margin table

Cost	82%	
Margin	18%	
Sales price	100%	£90

We know that the sales price of £90 represents 100%, so we can divide £90 by 100 to find 1%.

£90 / 100 = 0.90 or 90p

The margin is 18%.

£0.90 x 18 = £16.20

The cost is 82%

£0.90 x 82 = £73.80

Now we can put those into the table to check the figures.

Margin at 18%

Cost	82%	*£73.80*
Margin	18%	*£16.20*
Sales price	100%	£90

To check the figures:

Cost plus margin equals sales price.

£73.80 + £16.20 = £90

Chapter 2 – Tasks with worked answers

INCOMPLETE RECORDS

Task 1:

You are given the following information about a business.

Trade receivables at start of year	£3,000
Trade receivables at end of year	£6,000
Payments received to bank	£92,000
Discounts given to customers	£3,600
Sales	unknown

Use this information to reconstruct the sales ledger control account to find the missing sales figure.

Sales ledger control account / Trade receivables

Dr b/d	£	Cr	£
b/d	3000		92,000
	101600		3600
	98600		6000
	104600	b/d 6000	
	101600		101600

6000

Task 1: worked answer

You are given the following information about a business.

Trade receivables at start of year	£3,000
Trade receivables at end of year	£6,000
Payments received to bank	£92,000
Discounts given to customers	£3,600
Sales	unknown

Use this information to reconstruct the sales ledger control account to find the missing sales figure.

Workings and explanation:

The SLCA is an asset account because this the money that the business is owed by its customers. The balance b/d is a debit and the only other entry on the debit side is the sales on credit. All other entries will be credits.

The first step is to enter what we know.

Sales ledger control account / Trade receivables

Dr	£	Cr	£
Balance b/d	3,000	Bank payments received	92,000
Sales	?	Discounts allowed	3,600
		Balance c/d	6,000

Then we need to balance off the account to find the missing figure.

Total the credit side. Put the same figure on the debit side and deduct the debit entries to find the missing number.

92,000+3,600+6,000 = 101,600

101,600-3,000 = 98,600

The missing sales figure is £98,600.

You can see this in the table below.

Sales ledger control account / Trade receivables

Dr	£	Cr	£
Balance b/d	3,000	Bank payments received	92,000
Sales	98,600	Discounts allowed	3,600
		Balance c/d	6,000
	101,600		101,600
Balance b/d	6,000		

Task 2:

You have been provided with the information below.

Shaggy's business marks up its products by 40%. The sales for the year are £11,900.

Calculate the cost of the goods sold from this information by completing the table below.

Cost	100%	8500
% mark up	40%	3400
Sale	140%	11900 / 140%

Space for workings:

Task 2: **worked answer**

You have been provided with the information below.

Shaggy's business marks up its products by 40%. The sales for the year are £11,900.

Calculate the cost of the goods sold from this information.

We draw up the table for mark-up first. We know that cost is always 100% with mark-up and that the mark-up percentage is 40%. Therefore, sales will be 140%

Cost	100%	
Mark-up	40%	
Sales	140%	

Then we can add the sales figure that we know.

Cost	100%	
Mark-up	40%	
Sales	140%	£11,900

We take the sales figure of £11,900 and divide this by its percentage, then multiply by the mark-up percentage and then by the cost percentage.

£11,900 / 140 = £85

£85 = 1%

£85 x 40 = £3,400

£85 x 100 = £8,500

Then we add those numbers to the table to check our calculations.

Cost	100%	£8,500
Mark-up	40%	£3,400
Sales	140%	£11,900

To check our figures:

Cost plus mark-up equals sales price.

£8,500 + £3,400 = £11,900

Answer:
Cost of goods sold= £8,500

INCOMPLETE RECORDS

Task 3:

You have been given the following information about Lorna's business:

Sales ledger control account balance	A	£41,000
Purchase ledger control account balance	L	£13,000
Capital	C	£50,000
Bank (overdrawn balance)	L	£3,000
Closing inventory	A	£2,000
Drawings		£35,000
Accruals	L	£1,000
Loan outstanding	L	£4,000

Calculate the profit for the year using the net assets approach.

Remember that to use the net assets approach you need to apply the accounting equation.

Assets – liabilities = net assets

Or

Assets – liabilities = capital plus profit less drawings.

Remember that net assets is made up of capital plus profit less drawings.

Task 3: **worked answer**

You have been given the following information about Lorna's business:

Sales ledger control account balance	£41,000
Purchase ledger control account balance	£13,000
Capital	£50,000
Bank (overdrawn balance)	£3,000
Closing inventory	£2,000
Drawings	£35,000
Accruals	£1,000
Loan outstanding	£4,000

Calculate the profit for the year using the net assets approach.

Assets – liabilities = capital plus profit less drawings.

We need to work out where all these figures fit into the equation, so we start by finding all the assets and all the liabilities.

Assets

Assets are items that the business owns or are owed to it.

The sales ledger control is the balance of money OWED TO the business, so this is an asset.

Closing inventory is stock that the business OWNS, so this is an asset.

SLCA + closing inventory

£41,000 + £2,000 = £43,000

Liabilities

Liabilities are items that the business owes to others.

The purchase ledger control account is the balance of money OWED TO the suppliers, so this is a liability.

The overdrawn bank balance is money OWED TO the bank, so this is a liability.

Accruals is money that the business still OWES for expenses, so this is a liability.

The loan outstanding is money OWED TO the loan provider, so this is a liability.

PLCA + overdrawn bank balance + accruals + loan outstanding

£13,000 + £3,000 + £1,000 + £4,000 = £21,000

We can put this into the basic accounting equation like this:

Assets – liabilities = net assets

£43,000 – £21,000 = £22,000

Then we can separate the net assets:

Net assets = capital + profit − drawings

£22,000 = £50,000 + profit − £35,000

Profit was the missing figure, so we can use maths to find this missing figure by reversing the positive and negative numbers.

£22,000 − £50,000 + £35,000 = £7,000

Put this back into the calculation to check:

£22,000 = £50,000 + £7,000 − £35,000.

Answer: Profit = £7,000

Task 4:

Goldie runs a small sweet-shop and sell all her products for cash. She has provided a summary of her receipts and payments for the year but has not kept a record of her own drawings.

Cash in the till at the start of the year	£100
Cash received from customers	£38,000
Expenses paid with cash	£1,300
Rent paid with cash	£12,000
Cash banked	£8,000
Cash in the till at the end of the year	£150

Using this information draw up the cash account, clearly showing the drawings as the balancing figure.

INCOMPLETE RECORDS

Cash

Dr	£	Cr	£
b/d	100	Expenses	1300
received	38,000	Rent	12000
		cash banked	8000
		c/d	150
		Drawings	16650
	38100		38100

150

Task 4: **worked answer**

Goldie runs a small sweet-shop and sell all her products for cash. She has provided a summary of her receipts and payments for the year but has not kept a record of her own drawings.

Cash in the till at the start of the year	£100
Cash received from customers	£38,000
Expenses paid with cash	£1,300
Rent paid with cash	£12,000
Cash banked	£8,000
Cash in the till at the end of the year	£150

Using this information draw up the cash account, clearly showing the drawings as the balancing figure.

Workings and explanation:

Start by putting in the balance at the start of the year. Cash is an asset and according to DEAD CLIC, assets are debits, so we enter the balance brought down on the debit side.

Cash received from customers will increase the asset, so this is a debit too.

Expenses paid out of the cash account reduces the asset, so this is a credit.

Rent paid out of the cash account reduces the asset, so this is a credit.

Cash banked is also paid out of the cash account and reduces this asset, so this is a credit (and a debit in the bank account).

The cash in the till at the end of the year is the balance c/d so this is a credit as it will be a debit when it becomes the balance b/d in the next period.

The drawings figure is calculated by balancing the account. As it was the only missing number, we total the higher side, the debit side, put the same total on the credit side, then deduct all the credit entries to find the missing number.

To check this, it is always a good idea to total both sides again to make sure that they add up to the total of £38,100.

Cash

Debit	£	Credit	£
Balance b/d	100	Expenses	1,300
Sales	38,000	Rent	12,000
		Bank	8,000
		Drawings	16,650
		Balance c/d	150
	38,100		38,100
Balance b/d	150		

Chapter 3 – Tasks with answers in chapter 4

These questions are more complex and similar to exam style questions.

Task 5:

Nikev has provided you with the following information about his sole trader business.

Sales for the year	£136,000
Gross margin	25%
Opening inventory	£9,000
Closing inventory	£7,500

You are required to calculate the purchases for the year.

Hint

Whenever you see mark-up or margin mentioned, you know to draw up a table. In this task you will need to draw up the margin table to calculate the cost of sales.

Cost	75%	102,000
margin	25%	34,000
sales	100%	136,000

INCOMPLETE RECORDS

Then you will need to write out the trading account (the top part of the Statement of profit or loss). You will have one missing figure when you have done this, and that will be the purchases figure.

P + L

Sales	136,000	
Opening st	9000	
Purchases	102,000	
Closing st	(7500)	

Task 6:

You have the following information about Bluebell's sole trader business.

Bluebell transferred £15,000 of her own money into the business account to start the business.

Handwritten annotation: BANK — 15,000 | 2,000   CAPITAL — | 15,000 / 500 / 15500

Bluebell bought equipment for £2,000 which she paid for from the business bank account.

Handwritten annotation: EQUIP — 2000 / 500 / 2000   PLCA — | 2000

Bluebell brought tools into the business that she already owned to the value of £500.

Bluebell purchased tools on credit for £2,000.

Calculate the balance on Bluebell's capital account using this information.

Space for your workings is given on the next page.

Handwritten: £15500

Hint:

There will be some information that you do not need in this task. You are only looking for items that are relevant to the capital account.

Task 7:

Sharna is unsure whether some of her inventory or stock has been stolen during the year. She has provided you with the following information and asked if you could estimate the value of stock that has possibly been stolen.

Sales for the year	£480,000
Opening inventory at the start of the year	£28,000
Closing inventory at the end of the year	£9,000 *(19,000)*
Purchases for the year	£320,000 *(16,000)*
Gross profit margin	30%

Calculate the value of the stock that has potentially been stolen.

Handwritten margin table:

70	Cost	336,000
30		144,000
100	Sales	480,000

Hint:

You will need to draw up the margin table to calculate the cost of goods sold and then work out what the closing inventory figure should be as though this was a missing figure. Then compare this with the actual closing inventory to see if there is any stock missing.

3K

61

Task 8:

Libby has made sales during the year of £420,000 and uses 40% mark-up on cost to calculate her prices for goods. She has not kept a record of the cost of sales.

From this limited information, calculate the cost of sales figure and the gross profit for Libby.

Hint:

Draw up the mark-up table to answer this question.

100%	300,000	Cost
40%	120,000	mark up
140%	420000	sales

Space for workings:

Task 9:

Magda is a sole trader, and you are preparing her accounts for the year ended 31 December 2020.

You have been provided with the bank ledger and some further information:

Bank

Dr	£	Cr	£
Balance b/d	4,000	Office expenses	1,100
SLCA (from receivables)	42,000	Rent	2,400
		PLCA (to payables)	12,000
		Drawings	18,000
		Balance c/d	12,500
	46,000		46,000

The receivables balance at 1 Jan 2020 was £12,000.

The receivables balance at 31 Dec 2020 was £15,000.

The payables balance at 1 Jan 2020 was £8,000.

The payables balance at 31 Dec 2020 was £6,000.

There was accrued office expenses of £600 at 31 Dec 2020.

INCOMPLETE RECORDS

Note:

There are four parts to this question, so take it step by step.

a) Draw up the sales ledger control account, clearly showing the missing credit sales figure.

SLCA

Dr	£	Cr	£
b/d	12,000	Bank	42,000
	45,000		15,000
	57,000		57,000
	15,000		

Space for workings:

57000

b) Draw up the purchase ledger control account, clearly showing the missing credit purchases figure.

Dr	£	Cr	£
Bank	12,000	b/d	8000
		Purchase	10,000
c/d	6000		
	18,000		

Space for workings:

10K ✓

c) Calculate the capital figure at the start of the year.

Hint: Assets – liabilities = capital

Space for workings:

42,000
– 15,500
– 26,500

C + P – D
44,500 – 18,000

8K

d) Draw up a trial balance with the figures produced.

Remember: DEAD CLIC.

Ledger account	Dr	Cr
PLCA		6000 ~~18,000~~
SLCA	15,000	
Office Exp	1,700	
Rent	2,400	
Bank	42,500	
Drawings	18,000	~~18,000~~
Accrued Exp		600
Sales		
Purchases		
Capital		8,000

INCOMPLETE RECORDS

Task 10:

You have been provided with the following information about the VAT control account for Libby's sole trader business. You are working on the VAT records for the quarter ended 31 March 2021.

VAT on purchases   £270

VAT on sales   £830

Expenses paid including VAT   £360

VAT owing to HMRC on 1 Jan 2021 £420

a) Reconstruct the VAT control account, clearly showing the amount of VAT payable or reclaimable by Libby.

Space for workings:

INCOMPLETE RECORDS

VAT control account   march 31 2021

Dr	£	Cr	£
~~VAT on Purchases~~ VAT on Purchases	~~270~~ 270	~~VAT Owing~~ VAT Owing	~~420~~ 420 ✓
~~Expenses paid~~ Expenses paid	~~260~~ 260	~~VAT on Sales~~ VAT on Sales	~~830~~ 830 ✓
c/d	920		
	1250		1250
		b/d	920
			220

b) Identify whether the balance is owed to HMRC or is reclaimable.

Payable / Reclaimable

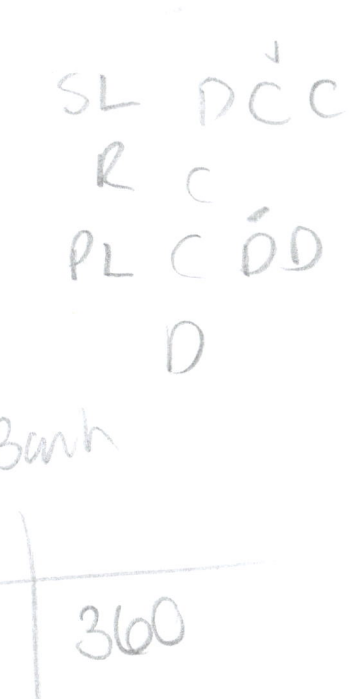

EXP

360

SL DCC
R C
PL C OD
   D

Bank

360

Task 11:

Charlotte has provided you with the following information.

Machinery	£260,000
Closing inventory	£90,000
Purchase ledger control account	£130,000
Sales ledger control account	£200,000
Bank balance (money in bank)	£23,000
Opening capital at 1 Jan 2020	£80,000
Bank loan outstanding	£38,000
Net profit	£280,000
Drawings	£15,000

Calculate how much capital has been introduced during the year.

There is space for workings on the next page.

Space for workings:

Machinery   260,000

Opening Capital   80,000

A − L = C

260,000
90,000
200,000
23,000
~~202,000~~
573,000

130,000
38,000
168,000

140,000
~~80,000~~
+ 280,000
− 15,000
= 405,000

INCOMPLETE RECORDS

Task 12:

a) The opening balance on the trade payables account was £900. The closing balance on the trade payables account was £1,300. Bank payments made to suppliers was £14,000. What was the value of the purchases?

Hint: Draw up the payables account.

PLCA

Dr	£	Cr	£
		c/d	900
Bank	14000		
		Purchases	14400
c/b	1300		~~1300~~

14400

b) Goods were purchased from the wholesaler for £4,000 and were sold to the public with a mark-up of 20%. What was the total value of the sales?

Hint: Use the mark-up table.

Purchases	4000	100 %
Mark up	800	20 %
Sales	4800	120 %

Space for workings:

INCOMPLETE RECORDS

c) Sales were £118,000 and the business uses a margin of 20%. What is the cost of goods sold figure?

Hint: Use the margin table.

		94,400
Purchase	80	~~8800~~ ~~94440~~
margin	20	23600
Sale	100	118000

Space for workings:

d) Goods are sold with a mark-up on cost of 25%. The sales figure is £7,500. Calculate the cost of sales.

Hint: Use the mark-up table.

Purchases	~~7500~~ 6000	100	6000
Markup	~~1875~~ 1500	25	1500
Sales	~~9375~~ 7500	125	

Space for workings:

Task 13:

Yogi is a sole trader, and you are working on his accounts for the year ended 31 December 2020. You have been provided with the following information.

Summary of bank transactions:

Money in bank at 1 January 2020	£22,500
Payments received from customers	£105,000
Total expenses paid	£16,000
Payments made to suppliers	£32,000
Money in bank at 31 December 2020	£79,500

Other information:

Receivables balance at 1 Jan 2020	£20,000
Receivables balance at 31 Dec 2020	£25,000
Payables balance at 1 Jan 2020	£15,500
Payables balance at 31 Dec 2020	£23,500

a) Calculate the opening capital.

Hint: Assets + liabilities = capital

Space for workings:

assets 1/Jan   Liability
22 500   15 500
20 000

= 27 000 CAPITAL

Bank

D	C
b/d 22 500	16 000
105 000	32 000

b/d 79 500

b) Prepare the SLCA showing the credit sales as the balancing figure.

Sales ledger control account

Dr	£	Cr	£
b/d	20,000	Bank	105,000
Sales	130,000		
		c/d	25,000
	130,000		130,000

c) Prepare the PLCA showing the credit purchases as the balancing figure.

Purchase ledger control account

Dr	£	Cr	£
Bank	32,000	b/d	15,500
		purchases	40,000
c/d	23,500		
	55,500		55,500
		b/d	23,500

d) Prepare a trial balance on 31 December 2020.

Ledger account	Debit	Credit
PLCA		23500
SLCA	~~30,000~~ 25,000	
Sales		110,000
Purchase	40,000	
Bank	79500	
EXP	16,000	
Capital		27,000

Space for workings:

INCOMPLETE RECORDS

Task 14:

a) Carly makes a 30% profit margin on her sale of handbags. Her opening inventory was £44,000, her closing inventory is £34,000 and her purchases were £130,000. Calculate her sales.

Hint: Draw up the margin table first, then use your answers to complete the trading account.

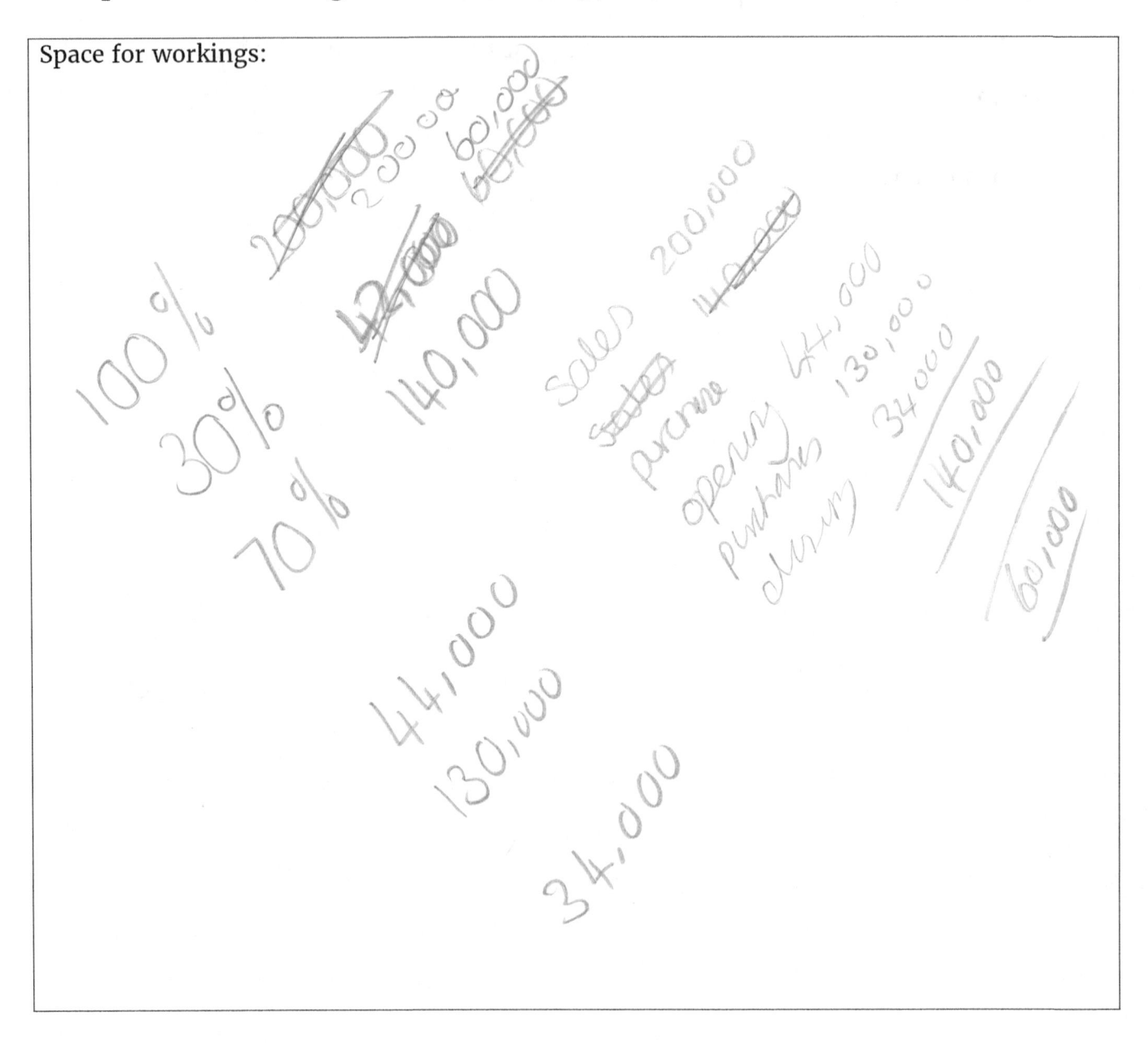

Space for workings:

b) Sheena makes a 40% profit margin on her sale of jewellery. Her sales totalled £200,000. Her opening inventory was £13,000, her closing inventory was £16,000. Her purchases were £127,000. Sheena is concerned that some of her inventory has been stolen. Calculate the value of inventory which has potentially been stolen.

Hint: Draw up the margin table first, then use your answers to complete the trading account leaving out the closing inventory in order to check the figure.

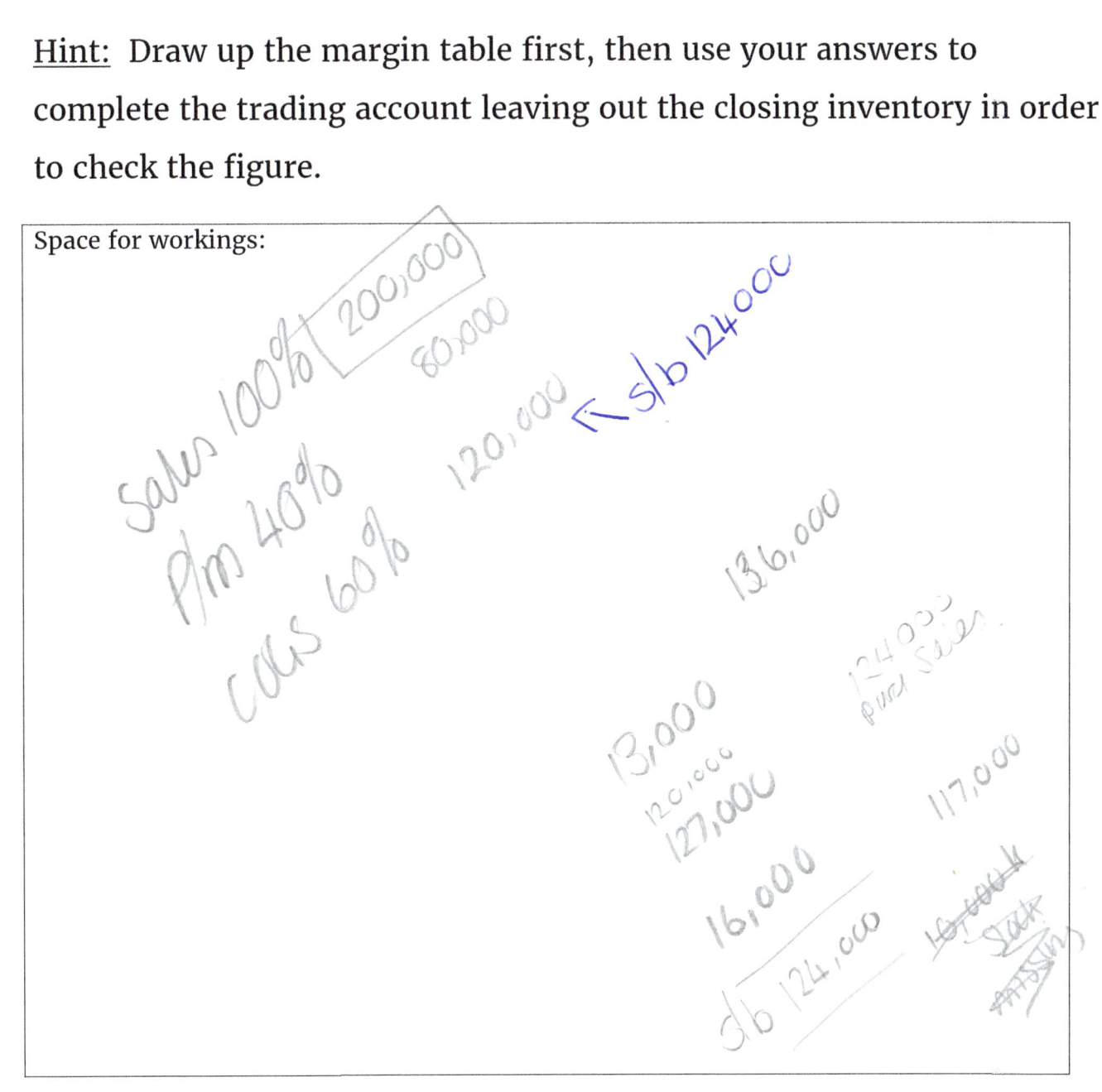

Space for workings:

Sales 100% 200,000 80,000
P/m 40%
COGS 60% 120,000 ← s/b 124,000

136,000

13,000
120,000
127,000

161,000

124,000 purch sales

117,000

c/b 124,000

stock missing

c) Ferhaan has supplied details about his receivables but has not kept a record of the discounts allowed. Reconstruct the receivables account clearly showing the discounts allowed as the balancing figure.

Balance at the start of the year £33,000

Payments received from customers £197,000

Sales on credit £222,000

Balance at the end of the year £38,000

Sales returns £8,000

Discounts allowed unknown

Trade receivables / SLCA

Dr	£	Cr	£
b/d	33,000	Bank	197,000
Sales	222,000	Discounts allowed	12,000
		Sales Returns	8,000
	255,000	c/d	38,000
b/d	38,000		

Task 15:

Renata buys in wooden tables and sells them for £345.00 each including VAT at 20%. She uses 25% mark-up to calculate her sales price.

What is the original cost of a table?

Hint: Note that there is VAT in this question.

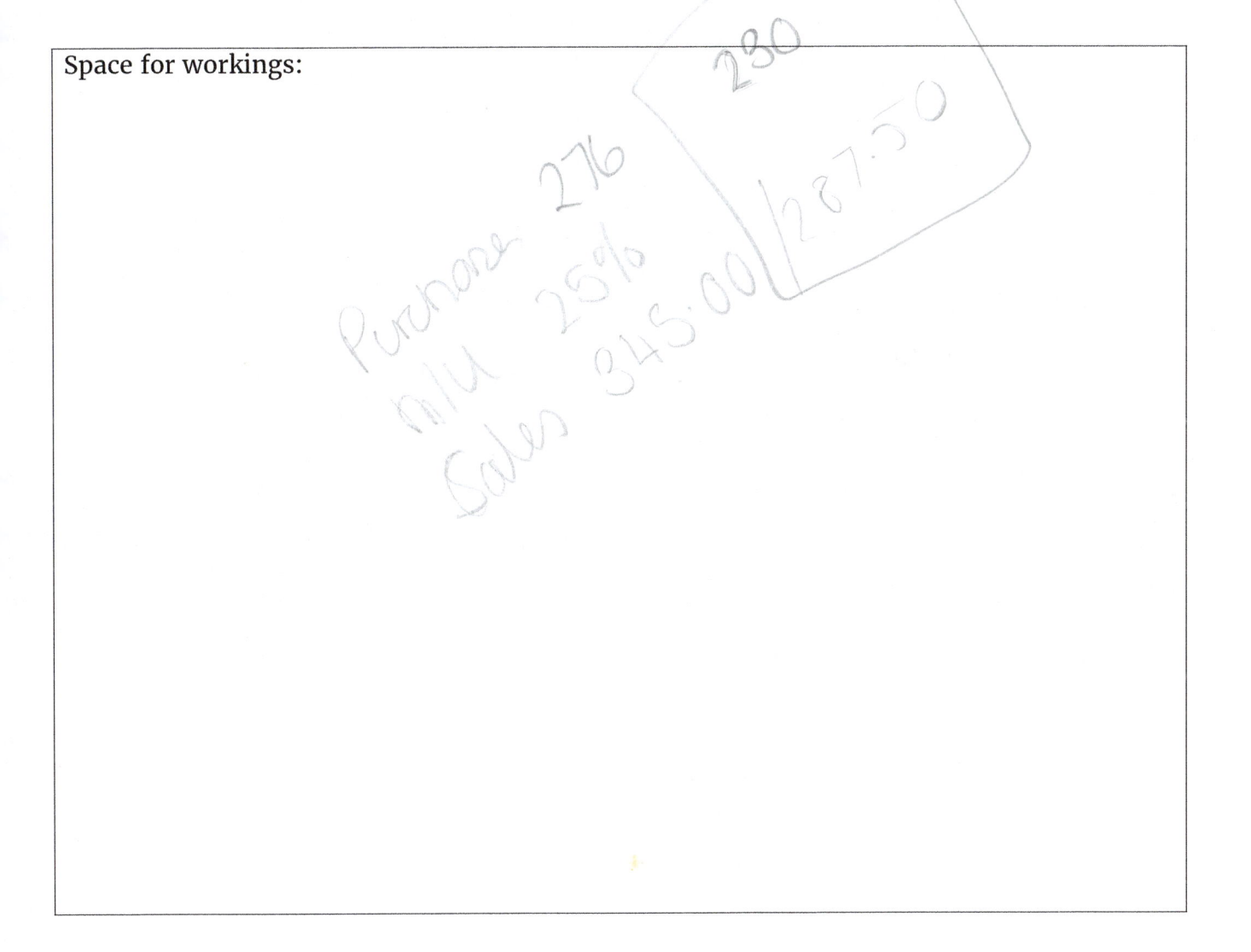

Space for workings:

Purchase 276
M/U 25%
Sales 345.00

280
287.50

Task 16:

Complete the table below by calculating the missing figures. The first line has been completed for you.

Cost £	Mark-up %	Net sales price £	VAT at 20% £	Gross sales price £
100.00	20	120.00	24.00	144.00
80.00	15	92.00	18.40	110.40
166.00	30	215.80	43.16	258.96
1090	40	1,526.00	305.20	1831.20
75.00	25%	93.75	18.75	112.50
33	45	47.85	9.57	57.42

There is space for workings on the next page.

Space for workings:

Task 17:

Complete the table below by calculating the missing figures. The first line has been completed for you.

Cost £	Margin %	Net sales price £	VAT at 20% £	Gross sales price £
160.00	20	200.00	40.00	240.00
	25	250.00	50.00	
525.00	30			900.00
	40	1500.00		1800.00
300.00	20			
800.00		1000.00		1200.00

There is space for workings on the next page.

INCOMPLETE RECORDS

Space for workings:

Task 18:

Indicate whether the following statements are true or false by ticking the appropriate box.

	True	False
A credit balance on the VAT control account indicates an amount owing to HMRC.	✓	
An amount owing to suppliers is shown as a credit in the purchase ledger control account.	✓	
Assets + liabilities = capital		✓
Trade payables is another way of describing the purchase ledger control account.	✓	
An amount owing from customers is shown as a debit in the purchase ledger control account.		✓
A debit balance in the bank ledger indicates an overdrawn balance.		✓
A payment from a customer is entered as a credit in the sales ledger control account.	✓	
Closing inventory is also known as closing stock.	✓	

INCOMPLETE RECORDS

	True	False
The sales ledger control account is also known as the trade payables account.		✓
VAT on sales is entered as a credit in the VAT control account.	✓	
The VAT on an irrecoverable debt is entered as a debit in the VAT control account.	✓	
Capital is a debit in the trial balance.		✓
Opening inventory + purchases − closing inventory = cost of sales.	✓	
A bank loan is a type of liability.	✓	
A refund of VAT received from HMRC is entered as a debit in the VAT control account.		✓
An item costs £100 and is marked up by 35%. The sales price is £135.	✓	

Chapter 4 – Answers

Task 5:

Nikev has provided you with the following information about his sole trader business.

Sales for the year	£136,000
Gross margin	25%
Opening inventory	£9,000
Closing inventory	£7,500

Calculate the purchases for the year.

Workings and explanation:

First step is to calculate the cost of sales and the margin figures using the margin table. Even though we have total sales and not unit price, we use the same method.

First enter what you know, and then fill in the missing numbers in the table.

Sales is 100% because this is a margin table and the other percentages are within the 100%.

We take the sales figure, divide it by 100 to find the value of 1% and then multiply it up by the margin percentage, 25 and the cost of sales percentage of 75.

(Sales / 100) x 25 = margin

(Sales / 100) x 75 = cost of sales

Cost	75%	£102,000
Margin	25%	£34,000
Sales price	100%	£136,000

With these figures we can draw up the trading account, which is the top part of the Statement of profit or loss.

Sales, less cost of sales = gross profit

Cost of sales is made up of opening inventory, plus purchases (our missing figure, less closing inventory.

INCOMPLETE RECORDS

The sales figure, cost of sales figure and margin figure from the table above are entered into the trading account. The opening and closing inventory balances from the information in the question are entered into the trading account.

Sales		£136,000
Cost of Sales:		
Opening inventory	£9,000	
Plus purchases	missing 102,000	
Less Closing inventory	(£7,500)	£102,000
Gross margin (gross profit)		£34,000

Note: Margin or Gross Margin = Gross Profit or Gross Profit Margin

We can work backwards now to find the missing purchases figure:

Cost of sales = opening inventory + purchases − closing inventory

£102,000 = £9,000 + purchases − £7,500

Turn it around: £9,000 − £7,500 + purchases = £102,000

£1,500 + purchases = £102,000

£1,500 + £100,500 = £102,000

Now the trading account can be re-drawn and we can double check the figures by calculating the cost of sales figure and deducting this from the sales figure, and this will give our gross profit.

Sales		£136,000
Cost of Sales:		
Opening inventory	£9,000	
Plus purchases	£100,500	
Less Closing inventory	(£7,500)	£102,000
Gross margin (gross profit)		£34,000

Task 6:

You have the following information about Bluebell's sole trader business.

Bluebell transferred £15,000 of her own money into the business account to start the business.

This is the initial money or capital introduced to start the business.

Bluebell bought equipment for £2,000 which she paid for from the business bank account.

This does not affect the capital account as it has been paid for by the business.

Bluebell brought tools into the business that she already owned to the value of £500.

This is capital as this is tools brought into the business, just the same as cash introduced into the business.

Bluebell purchased tools on credit for £2,000.

This does not affect the capital account as it will be paid for later by the business.

Calculate the balance on Bluebell's capital account using this information.

I always suggest that a T account is drawn for this type of question, but it is not necessarily required in the task.

Capital

Dr	£	Cr	£
		Bank	15,000
		Equipment	500
Balance c/d	15,500		
	15,500		15,500
		Balance b/d	15,500

Explanation:

The money introduced into the business is capital for the business, so this is entered on the credit side because capital is a credit according to DEAD CLIC.

The full journal entries for the transaction is:

Dr Bank   £15,000 (the bank balance is increasing)

Cr Capital £15,000

The equipment brought into the business was also a capital introduction as this was owned previously by the owner and they have 'given' it to the business for business use. This increases the capital balance on the credit side.

The journal entry for this is:

Dr Equipment £500 (the equipment balance/asset is increasing)

Cr Capital £500

The account is balanced by totalling the highest side, the credit side, putting the same number on the debit side, and then the calculating the missing figure on the debit side.

This is the balance to carry down, bal c/d. The balance is then brought down on the credit side.

The balance on the capital account is £15,500.

Task 7:

Sharna is unsure whether some of her inventory or stock has been stolen during the year. She has provided you with the following information and asked if you could estimate the value of stock that has possibly been stolen.

Sales for the year	£480,000
Opening inventory at the start of the year	£28,000
Closing inventory at the end of the year	£9,000
Purchases for the year	£320,000
Gross profit margin	30%

Calculate the value of the stock that has potentially been stolen.

Workings and explanation:

Draw up the margin table to work out the cost of sales and the gross profit margin/gross profit. Put in the information you know and then find the value of 1% before calculating the other figures.

Cost	70%	£336,000
Margin	30%	£144,000
Sales price	100%	£480,000

Draw up the trading account with the information given in the question and the figures calculated in the margin table, leaving out the closing stock/inventory figure.

Sales   £480,000

Cost of sales:

Opening inventory   £28,000

Plus purchases   £320,000

Less closing inventory   ????   £336,000

Gross profit margin   £144,000

Work out the missing closing inventory figure by reversing the positive and negative numbers, starting from the cost of sales figure.

£336,000 − £320,000 − £28,000 = −£12,000

Then put this back into the trading account to check all the figures.

Sales		£480,000
Cost of sales:		
Opening inventory	£28,000	
Plus purchases	£320,000	
Less closing inventory	£12,000	£336,000
Gross profit margin		£144,000

We have calculated that the closing stock or inventory figure should be £12,000.

Compare this to the physical inventory count provided by the business, which is £9,000.

£12,000 - £9,000 = £3,000.

It appears that £3,000 of stock is missing, possibly stolen.

Answer: £3,000

Task 8:

Libby has made sales during the year of £420,000 and uses 40% mark-up on cost to calculate her prices for goods. She has not kept a record of the cost of sales.

From this limited information, calculate the cost of sales figure and the gross profit for Libby.

Workings and explanation:

Draw up the mark-up table to work out the answers for this task. Mark-up goes up from 100% on cost, so cost is 100%, mark-up is 40% and the sales price is 140%.

Workings:

Sales value divided by 140 gives you the value of 1%, then multiply this by 40 for the mark-up and by 100 for the cost.

Sales = £420,000 = 140%

(Sales / 140) x 40 = mark-up

(Sales / 140) x 100 = cost

Note:

If you have a different method that works, use it. There is no right method, just the method that gets to the correct answer.

Cost	100%	£300,000
Mark-up	40%	£120,000
Sales price	140%	£420,000

The answer is £300,000.

Task 9:

Magda is a sole trader, and you are preparing her accounts for the year ended 31 December 2020.

You have been provided with the following information:

Bank

Dr	£	Cr	£
Balance b/d	4,000	Office expenses	1,100
SLCA (from receivables)	42,000	Rent	2,400
		PLCA (to payables)	12,000
		Drawings	18,000
		Balance c/d	12,500
	46,000		46,000

The receivables balance at 1 Jan 2020 was £12,000.

The receivables balance at 31 Dec 2020 was £15,000.

The payables balance at 1 Jan 2020 was £8,000.

The payables balance at 31 Dec 2020 was £6,000.

There was accrued office expenses of £600 at 31 Dec 2020.

a) Draw up the sales ledger control account, clearly showing the missing credit sales figure.

Explanation and workings:

Find the information that is relevant to the SLCA/receivables account and put those into the ledger, remembering that the missing figure will be the credit sales figure.

Remember: For the SLCA, the balance is an asset and so a debit and the only other debit is sales; everything else is a credit entry.

Balance off the account and work backwards to find the missing sales figure.

Sales ledger control account

Dr	£	Cr	£
Balance b/d	12,000	Bank (from receivables)	42,000
Sales (the missing figure)	45,000	Balance c/d	15,000
	57,000		57,000
Balance b/d	15,000		

b) Draw up the purchase ledger control account, clearly showing the missing credit purchases figure.

c) <u>Explanation and workings:</u>

Find the information that is relevant to the PLCA/Payables account and put those into the ledger, remembering that the missing figure will be the credit purchases figure.

Remember: For the PLCA, the balance is a liability and so a credit and the only other credit is purchases; everything else is a debit entry.

Balance off the account and work backwards to find the missing purchases figure.

Purchase ledger control account.

Dr	£	Cr	£
Bank (payments made)	12,000	**Balance b/d**	8,000
Balance c/d	6,000	**Purchases (the missing figure)**	10,000
	18,000		18,000
		Balance b/d	6,000

d) Calculate the capital figure at the start of the year.

Use the net assets approach here and the accounting equation:

You need to look at the starting figures provided in the question for this task.

Assets – Liabilities = Net assets

Net assets = Capital

Assets = SLCA balance and bank balance

Liabilities = PLCA balance

Assets = £12,000 (taken from information supplied) + £4,000 (taken from balance in bank account summary

Assets = £16,000

Liabilities = £8,000 (taken from the information supplied)

Assets – liabilities = capital

£16,000 − £8,000 = £8,000

Capital = £8,000

e) Draw up a trial balance with the figures produced.

Ledger account	DR	CR
Sales ledger control account	15,000	
Purchase ledger control account		6,000
Bank	12,500	
Accrued expenses		600
Drawings	18,000	
Capital		8,000
Office expenses	1,700	
Rent	2,400	
Sales		45,000
Purchases	10,000	
Totals	59,600	59,600

The SLCA balance, the PLCA balance and the accrued expenses were taken from the information supplies. The bank balance was taken from the bank summary, as was the drawings and rent. The office expenses were adjusted with the accrued expenses of £600. The sales and purchases figures were taken from the SLCA and PLCA drawn up earlier in the task.

Well done if you got through this one first time, but don't worry if you didn't. It is tricky and more difficult that most Level 3 exam questions.

Task 10:

You have been provided with the following information about the VAT control account for Libby's sole trader business. You are working on the VAT records for the quarter ended 31 March 2021.

VAT on purchases   £270

VAT on sales   £830

Expenses paid including VAT   £360

VAT owing to HMRC on 1 Jan 2021   £420

a) Reconstruct the VAT control account, clearly showing the amount of VAT payable or reclaimable by Libby.

Workings and explanation:

When reconstructing the VAT account remember that a credit is a liability, and a debit is an asset. VAT on sales is payable to HMRC so this is a credit. VAT on purchases is reclaimed from HMRC so this is a debit.

Note that the expenses figure is including VAT, so you need to find the VAT element for the VAT control account.

Total expenses = £360 including VAT

£360 divided by 120 is 1%.

1% = £3

Multiply this by 20 for the VAT element.

£3 x 20 = £60

Another way of remembering what sides the VAT goes is to remember that sales are a credit, so the VAT on sales is a credit; purchases are a debit, so the VAT on purchases is a debit; expenses are a debit, so the VAT on expenses are a debit and so on.

The balance b/d is on the credit side, and this represents an amount payable to HMRC, so this is a liability.

VAT control account

Dr	£	Cr	£
VAT on purchases	270	Balance b/d	420
VAT on expenses	60	VAT on sales	830
Balance c/d	920		
	1,250		1,250
		Balance b/d	920

b) Identify whether the balance is owed to HMRC or is reclaimable.

Payable / ~~Reclaimable~~

This is payable because the balance b/d is on the credit side, which means this is a liability.

Task 11:

Charlotte has provided you with the following information.

Machinery	£260,000
Closing inventory	£90,000
Purchase ledger control account	£130,000
Sales ledger control account	£200,000
Bank balance (money in bank)	£23,000
Opening capital at 1 Jan 2020	£80,000
Bank loan outstanding	£38,000
Net profit	£280,000
Drawings	£15,000

Calculate how much capital has been introduced during the year.

Workings and explanation:

To answer this question, we need to use the accounting equation.

Assets – liabilities = net assets

Net assets = capital + profit – drawings

The assets are things that the business owns or are owed to it.

Assets: Machinery, closing inventory, SLCA, bank balance

The liabilities are amounts that the business owes to others.

Liabilities: PLCA, bank loan

Assets – Liabilities = net assets

£573,000 – £168,000 = £405,000

We can identify each item from the table to make this easier to see. The assets are added together. The liabilities are added together.

The liabilities are deducted from the assets to give the net assets figure.

Machinery	£260,000	asset
Closing inventory	£90,000	asset
Purchase ledger control account	£130,000	liability
Sales ledger control account	£200,000	asset
Bank balance (money in bank)	£23,000	asset
Opening capital at 1 Jan 2020	£80,000	capital
Bank loan outstanding	£38,000	liability
Net profit	£280,000	profit
Drawings	£15,000	drawings

The net assets figure of £405,000 is broken down into capital, profit and drawings in the accounting equation.

Net assets = capital + profit − drawings

£405,000 = capital + £280,000 − £15,000

£405,000 = £280,000 − £15,000 + capital

£405,000 = £265,000 + £140,000

The question asked us how much capital has been introduced during the year.

To work out how much capital has been introduced during the year we have to look at the opening capital and find the difference between the opening and closing capital.

Opening capital was £80,000

Closing capital was £140,000

Therefore, the capital introduced during the year is £60,000.

Task 12:

a) The opening balance on the trade payables account was £900. The closing balance on the trade payables account was £1,300. Bank payments made to suppliers was £14,000. What was the value of the purchases?

Workings and explanation:

The opening balance on the payables account is a liability so this is the balance b/d on the credit side. Remember that the only other credit will be purchases which is our missing figure. The bank payments made came out of the bank as a credit and reduce the trade payables account as a debit. The balance c/d is a debit because this will be brought down on the debit side in this liability account. Balance off the account to find the missing purchases figure.

PLCA / Trade payables

Dr	£	Cr	£
Bank	14,000	Balance b/d	900
Balance c/d	1,300	Purchases	14,400
	15,300		15,300
		Balance b/d	1,300

b) Goods were purchased from the wholesaler for £4,000 and were sold to the public with a mark-up of 20%. What was the total value of the sales?

Workings and explanation:

You may have answered this question without the table.

£4,000 is cost and we mark-up from cost, so add 20% to the cost to get the sales figure which is 120%.

£4,000 x 20% = £800

£4,000 + £800 = £4,800

Or you may have drawn up the mark-up table like this.

£4,000 divided by 100 = 1%

£40 = 1%

£40 x 20 = £800

£40 x 120 = £4,800

Cost	100%	£4,000
Mark-up	20%	£800
Sales	120%	£4,800

c) Sales were £118,000 and the business uses a margin of 20%. What is the cost of goods sold figure?

Workings and explanation:

It is always a good idea to draw up the table to avoid errors with this type of question. Margin is "within" 100%, so the sales figure is the 100%, the margin is 20% and the cost is 80%.

Sales = 100%, so total sales divided by 100 will give the value of 1%.

Then multiply this by 20 for the margin and by 80 for the cost.

Cost	80%	£94,400
Margin	20%	£23,600
Sales	100%	£118,000

d) Goods are sold with a mark-up on cost of 25%. The sales figure is £7,500. Calculate the cost sales.

Workings and explanation:

Again, drawing up the table helps to avoid errors. Mark-up goes "up" from 100%, so cost is 100%, mark-up is 25% and sales is 125%.

As we know the sales figure, divide the sales by the sales percentage and then multiply up with the cost percentage and the mark-up percentage to complete the table.

(£7,500/125) x 100 = £6,000

(£7,500/125) x 100 = £1,500

Cost	100%	£6,000
Mark-up	25%	£1,500
Sales	125%	£7,500

Task 13:

Yogi is a sole trader and you are working on his accounts for the year ended 31 December 2020. You have been provided with the following information.

Summary of bank transactions:

Money in bank on 1 January 2020	£22,500
Payments received from customers	£105,000
Total expenses paid	£16,000
Payments made to suppliers	£32,000
Money in bank at 31 December 2020	£79,500

Other information:

Receivables balance at 1 Jan 2020	£20,000
Receivables balance at 31 Dec 2020	£25,000
Payables balance at 1 Jan 2020	£15,500
Payables balance at 31 Dec 2020	£23,500

a) Calculate the opening capital.

Workings and explanation:

Money in the bank and the trade receivables are both assets.

Trade payables are a liability.

Assets – liabilities = capital.

£22,500 + £20,000 – £15,500 = £27,000

The opening capital was £27,000.

b) Prepare the SLCA showing the credit sales as the balancing figure.

Workings and explanation:

Remember that the SLCA is an asset, so the balance b/d and sales will be debit entries and everything else goes on the credit side. The sales figure is the missing figure, so we balance the account to calculate the missing figure.

Sales ledger control account

Dr	£	Cr	£
Balance b/d	20,000	Bank (payments received)	105,000
Sales	110,000	Balance c/d	25,000
	130,000		130,000
Balance b/d	25,000		

c) Prepare the PLCA showing the credit purchases as the balancing figure.

Workings and explanation:

Remember that the PLCA is a liability, so the balance b/d and purchases will be credit entries and everything else goes on the debit side. The purchases figure is the missing figure, so we balance the account to calculate the missing figure.

Purchase ledger control account

Debit	£	Credit	£
Bank (payments made)	32,000	Balance b/d	15,500
Balance c/d	23,500	Purchases	40,000
	55,500		55,500
		Balance b/d	23,500

d) Prepare a trial balance on 31 December 2020.

Ledger account	Debit	Credit
Bank	79,500	
SLCA	25,000	
PLCA		23,500
Sales		110,000
Purchases	40,000	
Capital		27,000
Expenses	16,000	
Totals	160,500	160,500

Task 14:

a) Carly makes a 30% profit margin on her sale of handbags. Her opening inventory was £44,000, her closing inventory is £34,000 and her purchases were £130,000. Calculate her sales.

Workings and explanation:

First, we must calculate the sales, cost of sales and margin figures using a margin table.

We are only given the workings for the cost of sales, so we need to work this out first.

Opening inventory + purchases – closing inventory = cost of sales

£44,000 + £130,000 - £34,000 = £140,000

Now we have the cost of sales figure, we can put that in the table first then calculate the other figures from that.

We only know the cost of sales amount and the margin percentage, so start with those and then add in the other percentages before calculating the amounts for sales and margin.

Cost	70%	£140,000
Margin	30%	£60,000
Sales	100%	£200,000

As this was a margin table, we knew that the sales figure was 100% and the other percentages were within the 100. The question told us that the margin was 30%, so we can work out the cost percentage is 70%.

From that we can take the cost of sales figure, divide it by its associated percentage, 70, to find the value of 1% and then multiply by 30 for the margin and 100 for the sales figre.

(£140,000/70) x 30 = £60,000

(£140,000/70) x 100 = £200,000

The answer is £200,000.

b) Sheena makes a 40% profit margin on her sale of jewellery. Her sales totalled £200,000. Her opening inventory was £13,000, her closing inventory was £16,000. Her purchases were £127,000. Sheena is concerned that some of her inventory has been stolen. Calculate the value of inventory which has potentially been stolen.

Workings and explanation:

When faced with a question where they are asking you to check a figure, you need to treat that as the missing figure to start with. Then when you have calculated what it should be, then you can compare it with the one given by Sheena.

We calculate the margin and cost of sales using the margin table. We know the sales figure and the margin percentage, so we start with those and then complete the rest of the table.

Cost	60%	£120,000
Margin	40%	£80,000
Sales	100%	£200,000

Then we draw up the trading account, treating the closing inventory as the missing figure.

Sales   £200,000

Cost of sales:

Opening inventory   £13,000

Plus purchases   £127,000

Less closing inventory   (??)   £120,000

Gross profit margin   £80,000

We work backwards to calculate the closing inventory figure and complete the trading account:

Sales   £200,000

Cost of sales:

Opening inventory   £13,000

Plus purchases   £127,000

Less closing inventory (£20,000)   £120,000

Gross profit margin   £80,000

We have calculated the closing stock as £20,000. We can compare that to the figure that Sheena gave us to see if any stock has potentially been stolen.

Closing inventory figure provided by Sheena was £16,000.

Closing inventory figure calculated is £20,000.

This means that the amount of inventory that has potentially been stolen is £4,000.

c) Ferhaan has supplied details about his receivables but has not kept a record of the discounts allowed. Reconstruct the receivables account clearly showing the discounts allowed as the balancing figure.

Balance at the start of the year   £33,000

Payments received from customers £197,000

Sales on credit   £222,000

Balance at the end of the year   £38,000

Sales returns   £8,000

Discounts allowed   unknown

Workings and explanation:

The receivables account is the sales ledger control account (SLCA). The balance on the SLCA is an asset and the only other debit entry is more sales on credit, increasing the value of the asset. Everything else will be a credit reducing the value of the asset. Enter all the transactions into the ledger and the balancing figure will be the missing discounts allowed figure.

SLCA

Debit	£	Credit	£
Balance b/d	33,000	Bank (payments rec'd)	197,000
Sales on credit	222,000	Sales returns	8,000
		Discounts allowed	12,000
		Balance c/d	38,000
	255,000		255,000
Balance b/d	38,000		

Task 15:

Renata buys in wooden tables and sells them for £345.00 each including VAT at 20%. She uses 25% mark-up to calculate her sales price.

What is the original cost of a table?

Hint: Note that there is VAT in this question.

Workings and explanation:

The table is sold for £345.00 including VAT, so we first need to remove the VAT to find the net price.

You can do this in a number of ways, but here are a couple of suggestions if you need help.

£345 divided by 6 = VAT amount

£345 divided by 120, then multiplied by 20 = VAT amount

£345 divided by 120, then multiplied by 100 = net amount.

Net amount is £287.50.

Now we need to draw up the mark-up table with this information.

We know that the mark-up is 25%, so we can enter that. We are using mark-up, so cost is 100%. This means that sales are 125%. We also know that the net sales price of a table is £287.50, so this goes into the table.

The sales price is divided by its associated percentage of 125 to find the value of 1%, then multiplied by 25 for the mark-up and by 100 for the cost.

Cost	100%	£230.00
Mark-up	25%	£57.50
Sales	125%	£287.50

The cost of the table is £230.00

Task 16:

Complete the table below by calculating the missing figures. The first line has been completed for you.

Cost £	Mark-up %	Net sales price £	VAT at 20% £	Gross sales price £
100.00	20	120.00	24.00	144.00
80.00	15	92.00	**18.40**	**110.40**
166.00	30	**215.80**	**43.16**	258.96
1,090.00	40	1,526.00	305.20	**1,831.20**
75.00	**25**	93.75	18.75	**112.50**
33.00	45	**47.85**	9.57	57.42

Workings and explanations:

Net sales price of £92, plus VAT at 20% = £18.40

Net sales price plus VAT = gross sales price. £110.40

£166 plus mark-up at 30%.

It is still just as quick to draw up the table.

Cost	100%	£166.00
Mark-up	30%	£49.80
Sales	130%	£215.80

Or you may have just taken £166 and multiplied by 30% for the mark-up.

£166 x 30% = £49.80. Then added this to your cost price.

£166 + £49.80 = £215.80.

For the VAT, we multiply that by 20%.

£215.80 x 20% = £43.16

To check that, we can add the net sales price and the VAT together and they should give us the gross sales price shown in the table.

£215.80 + £43.16 = £258.96

The next one gives us the net sale price and the VAT and not the gross sales price, so we can just add those two together for the gross sale price.

£1,526.00 + £305.20 = £1,831.20

Then we need to work back to find the original cost.

The net sales price is £1,526.00 and the mark-up is 40%, so we can draw the mark-up table to find the cost.

£1,526.00 is the sales price, so we divide it by its associated percentage of 140 to find the value of 1%, then multiply by 40% for the mark-up and by 100 for the cost.

Cost	100%	£1,090.00
Mark-up	40%	£436.00
Sales	140%	£1,526.00

£75 is the cost for the next one and £93.75 is the net sales price. We need to calculate the mark-up for this one, so again the mark-up table can be used.

We know that cost is 100%, so we can put that in, but we don't know any other percentages.

The mark-up value can be calculated by taking the sales price and deducting the cost. £93.75 + £75.00 = £18.75

Cost	100%	£75.00
Mark-up		£18.75

Sales		£93.75

We know that the cost is £75.00 and this is 100%, so we can find 1% by dividing £75 by 100.

£75.00 / 100 = £0.75

To work out the percentage associated with these amounts we can divide the totals by the percentage amount like this:

Mark-up is £18.75. Divide this by £0.75 = 25

Sales is £96.75. Divide this by £0.75 = 125

These are the missing percentages for mark-up and sales.

Cost	100%	£75.00
Mark-up	25%	£18.75
Sales	125%	£93.75

For the final one, you can use a similar approach. The net sales figure is the gross sales figure less the VAT.

£57.42 - £9.57 = £47.85

The missing figure is the cost, so we can draw the mark-up table to find this.

Cost	100%	£33.00
Mark-up	45%	£14.85
Sales	145%	£47.85

The cost is 100%, the mark-up is 45%, so the sales price is 145%.

Take the sales figure of £47.85, divide by 145 to find the value of 1%, then multiply by 100 for the cost and by 45 for the mark-up.

£47.85 / 145 = £0.33

x 45 = £14.85

x 100 = £33.00

Task 17:

Complete the table below by calculating the missing figures. The first line has been completed for you.

Cost £	Margin %	Net sales price £	VAT at 20% £	Gross sales price £
160.00	20	200.00	40.00	240.00
187.50	25	250.00	50.00	**300.00**
525.00	30	**750.00**	**150.00**	900.00
900.00	40	1500.00	**300.00**	1800.00
300.00	20	**375.00**	**75.00**	**450.00**
800.00	**20**	1000.00	**200.00**	1200.00

Workings and explanations:

The sales price is £250, and the margin is 25%, so we can draw the table to find the missing cost figure. Remember that the sales figure is 100% and the other percentages are within this.

We divide the sales price of £250 by 100 and then multiply by 25 for the margin, and by 75 for the cost.

Cost	75%	£187.50
Margin	25%	£62.50
Sales	100%	£250.00

To find the missing gross sales figure, we just add the net sales price and the VAT together.

Next, we are given the cost figure and the margin percentage, so we put these into the table to find the net sales price. The sales price is 100%, the margin is 30%, so the cost must be 70%.

We take the cost price of £525, divide by 70 and multiply by 30 for the margin and by 100 for the sales price.

Cost	70%	£525.00
Margin	30%	£225.00
Sales	100%	£750.00

Now we have the net sales price, we add the VAT by multiply this by 20%. To check this, we make sure that the net sales price and the VAT price equal the gross sales figure provided.

Now we are given the net sales price and the margin percentage, so we draw up the table for this one to find the missing margin and cost figures.

Cost	60%	£900.00
Margin	40%	£600.00
Sales	100%	£1,500.00

The missing VAT amount can be calculated by taking £1,500 and multiplying by 20%. This can be checked by adding the net sales price to the VAT to make sure it gives the gross sales price shown in the table.

In the next one, we are only given the cost of £300 and the margin percentage of 20% and need to complete the rest of the table.

We start by drawing the margin table to find the net sales price, then add 20% to this to find the sales price.

Cost	80%	£300.00
Margin	20%	£75.00
Sales	100%	£375.00

The final one gives us the cost and the net sales price, but no margin percentage, so we need to find this using the table. We can add the amounts in first because we know the cost price and the sales price, so the margin is the difference between the two.

We know that the sales price represents 100%.

We can divide the sales price by 100 to find the value of 1%.

£1,000 / 100 = £10

£10 = 1%

Now we can divide £200 by £10 to find how many percent are contained in that figure. £200 / £10 = 20. The margin percentage is 20%

We can divide the £800 by £10 to find how many percent are contained in that figure. £800 / £10 = 80. The cost percentage is 80%.

Cost	80%	£800.00
Margin	20%	£200.00
Sales	100%	£1,000.00

The VAT on the net sales price can be calculated by multiplying £1,000 by 20% and checked by adding the net sales price and the VAT together.

Task 18:

Indicate whether the following statements are true or false by ticking the appropriate box.

	True	False
A credit balance on the VAT control account indicates an amount owing to HMRC.	✓	
An amount owing to suppliers is shown as a credit in the purchase ledger control account.	✓	
Assets + liabilities = capital		✓
Trade payables is another way of describing the purchase ledger control account.	✓	
An amount owing from customers is shown as a debit in the purchase ledger control account.		✓
A debit balance in the bank ledger indicates an overdrawn balance.		✓
A payment from a customer is entered as a credit in the sales ledger control account.	✓	
Closing inventory is also known as closing stock.	✓	

INCOMPLETE RECORDS

	True	False
The sales ledger control account is also known as the trade payables account.		✓
VAT on sales is entered as a credit in the VAT control account.	✓	
The VAT on an irrecoverable debt is entered as a debit in the VAT control account.	✓	
Capital is a debit in the trial balance.		✓
Opening inventory + purchases – closing inventory = cost of sales.	✓	
A bank loan is a type of liability.	✓	
A refund of VAT received from HMRC is entered as a debit in the VAT control account.		✓
An item costs £100 and is marked up by 35%. The sales price is £135.	✓	

Explanations:

A credit balance on the VAT control account indicates an amount owing to HMRC as this is a liability.

An amount owing to suppliers is shown as a credit in the PLCA as this is a liability.

Assets − liabilities = capital and not assets + liabilities = capital.

Trade payables is another way of describing the PLCA.

An amount owing from customers is shown as a debit in the sales ledger control account, not the purchase ledger control account.

A debit balance in the bank ledger indicates an asset, so money in the bank, not an overdrawn balance as this would be a liability.

A payment from a customer is entered as a credit in the SLCA as it was a debit in the bank.

Closing inventory means the same as closing stock.

The sales ledger control account is also known as the trade receivables account, not the trade payables account.

VAT on sales is entered as a credit as this is a liability, money owed to HMRC.

VAT on an irrecoverable debt is a debit as this is VAT to be reclaimed from HMRC, an asset.

Capital is a credit in the trial balance, not a debit, because this is money owed back to the owner of the business, a liability.

Opening inventory + purchases −closing inventory is the correct calculation for cost of sales.

A bank loan is a type of liability because it is money owed to the bank.

A refund of VAT from HMRC is a credit because it was a debit in the bank, or because it reduces the amount that HMRC owes the business.

An item costing £100 and marked up by 35% will have a sales price of £135.

INCOMPLETE RECORDS

I hope you have found this workbook useful. If you have any comments, you can find me on my Facebook page: Teresa Clarke Accountancy Tutoring.

You might also like to try my other workbooks, links for all of which can be found here.

https://www.teresaclarke.co.uk/books/

Teresa Clarke FMAAT

Printed in Great Britain
by Amazon